DATE DUE

THE INGLIS LECTURE

1955

INGLIS LECTURES
IN SECONDARY EDUCATION

"…the last best hope…"

DEMOCRACY MAKES NEW DEMANDS

ON EDUCATION

"...the last best hope..."

DEMOCRACY MAKES NEW DEMANDS

ON EDUCATION

HENRY WYMAN HOLMES

HARVARD UNIVERSITY PRESS

CAMBRIDGE

1955

LIBRARY OF CONGRESS CATALOG CARD NUMBER 55–10973
PRINTED IN THE UNITED STATES OF AMERICA

To

John J. Mahoney

primus inter pares

in a

Pioneering Venture

in

Civic Education

. . . that which we are, we are;—
One equal temper of heroic hearts,
Made weak by time and fate, but strong in will
To strive, to seek, to find, and not to yield.

—Tennyson

THE INGLIS LECTURESHIP

To honor the memory of Alexander Inglis, 1879–1924, his friends and colleagues gave to the Graduate School of Education, Harvard University, a fund for the maintenance of a Lectureship in Secondary Education. To the study of problems in this field Professor Inglis devoted his professional career, leaving as a precious heritage to his co-workers the example of his industry, intellectual integrity, human sympathy, and social vision. It is the purpose of the Lectureship to perpetuate the spirit of his labors and contribute to the solution of problems in the field of his interest. The lectures on this foundation are published annually by the School.

"...the last best hope..."

DEMOCRACY MAKES NEW DEMANDS ON EDUCATION

THE TITLE OF THIS LECTURE—"the last best hope"—is part of a sentence in Lincoln's message to the Congress at one of the darkest periods of our Civil War—December 1862: "We shall nobly save, or meanly lose, the last best hope of earth."

I

In these simple words Lincoln lifted a domestic conflict from its temporal and local setting to the plane of permanent significance for all mankind. He did so repeatedly, as in the Gettysburg Address and in his letter of September 1863 to the Unionists in Springfield, Illinois, in which he thanked the Federal forces " . . . for the great republic—for the principle it lives by, and keeps alive—for man's vast future . . ."

No doubt there were others who understood the fate that rode upon the Union arms, but it was Lincoln who had the strange, exciting power to put the full meaning of a dire, almost unendurable, crisis into common speech. As the *New*

York Times said of his Springfield letter, it contained "not a word which was not familiar to the plainest plowman."

Who can doubt the need to put great issues into simple words? Are not the deepest questions those that touch most lives? In education, therefore, is there not a task to which some teachers must devote themselves unceasingly—from which no teacher quite escapes: the task of giving clarity and power to the broadest and most human ends of learning?

This task is anything but easy. The temptation is to moralize instead of building up the facts and setting forth the problems so that higher goals of action are revealed. And with slower minds, the temptation is to give up teaching anything at all that has significance beyond the narrow round of personal interest. The demagogue, and those who vulgarize the press, TV, and radio, cast doubt upon the power of the common mind to understand a public issue, anyway. Lincoln had no such doubt.

In Benjamin Thomas's masterful new life of the Great Emancipator occur these sentences:

Lincoln's human dealings had given him fixity of purpose. Time and again, in one crisis after another, he had seen the judgments of supposedly great minds turn out to be so utterly mistaken that they would have brought ruin beyond retrieving if he had followed them. The people's composite wisdom and moral rectitude had proved to be surer guides, and he had deferred to mass opinion, firm in the conviction that the people were trustworthy, when informed . . . His conduct had been essentially Christian. He conformed to the teachings of the Golden Rule and the Sermon on the Mount, not self-righteously or sanctimoniously, but because he learned that Christian virtues are democratic virtues, too, in offering men a means of living together in dignity, equality, and mutual respect.[1]

I can not rid myself of the conviction that Abraham Lincoln's feeling about the people ought long ago to have made more difference in education than it ever has and that it ought to make more difference now than prevalent educational thinking is adventurous enough to urge.

Lincoln believed, as Mr. Thomas tells us, and as Lincoln said himself, that the people are "trustworthy, *when informed* [italics mine]." Perhaps he knew—he studied closely many writings of the Founding Fathers—that challenging statement of Jefferson's: "I know no safe depository of the ultimate powers of society but the people themselves; and if we think them not enlightened enough to exercise their control with a whole-

---

[1] Benjamin P. Thomas, *Abraham Lincoln.* Copyright 1952 by Benjamin P. Thomas. Published by Alfred A. Knopf, Inc., 1952. Pages 496–497.

some direction, the remedy is not to take it from them, but to inform their discretion through education."

Lincoln, of course, could not afford to wait for anything that schools might do; he had to trust to mass opinion on questions so immense and pressing that his best recourse was to his own exceptional command of language. We look back, gratefully and with wonder, at his power to reveal a vision to which thousands turned in suffering and sacrifice. Must we not ask ourselves if there is not something more that schools can do to keep that vision clear and glowing in the minds and hearts of young Americans? Must we not think through, again and yet again, the meaning of democracy and feel it deeply in its application to the problems of our day, bringing it to bear in all our teaching, wherever and when-ever we can?

Must the schools stand hesitant and fearful before public issues, always waiting for new Lincolns who will trust the people and help them look beyond the moment? The logic of events may work but darkly in the minds of those who listen to divided counsel in high places. Meanwhile mass opinion is anxiously consulted every day, until among us there are those who speak of it with fear. If any institution "works at the grass roots," it is the school. There must be something schools can do—and something more, and more direct, than many schools are doing now—to render mass opinion a compelling force for wisdom, or at least to make it more responsive to wise leadership.

Our thinking about education has concerned itself too little with the common mind—that is, with what is needed and attainable for all alike. We talk too much about *"the* educated man," a paragon of nicely balanced, highly trained abilities and moral traits, whose "liberal education" has produced a "rounded" or an "integrated" personality.

It is as if we were rewording that majestic but altogether futile definition of education given by Milton in his *Tractate:* "I call therefore a compleat and generous Education that which fits a man to perform justly, skilfully, and magnanimously all the offices, both private and publick, of Peace and War."

No such education is possible; no individual who could be so educated exists. There is no choice of subject, method, discipline, or regimen by which to mould the perfect man. Society must get along without him. At the root of democracy lies the acceptance of individual differences, and education has been learning slowly how to make enough allowance for them. Education must deal with the infinite variety of imperfect human beings who can nevertheless be helped by education to live together well.

A crucial part of that undertaking, and the hardest part, is to define and make secure the limits of the individual's freedom. Freedom without limits is a fake. Yet neither law nor science can impose the rules that make good morals or good manners certain, not to speak of self-denying effort. If we are to educate for freedom, we must go beyond negations, whether of the courts, the family, or the church, and seek the only final guarantee of human progress and achievement—willing coöperation on the part of great numbers of free men and women in constructive work for ends beyond survival.

"The end of human society," wrote Whitehead, in *Adventures of Ideas*, "is to elicit . . . psychic energies . . . A Barbarian speaks in terms of power. He dreams of the superman with the mailed fist . . . ultimately his final good is one will imposing itself on other wills. The Periclean [i.e., the democratic] ideal is action weaving itself into a texture of persuasive beauty analagous to the delicate splendor of nature." [2]

Is it incongruous to quote from Whitehead, a metaphysician, in a discourse which takes its start from the simplicities of Lincoln's thought

---

[2]Alfred North Whitehead, *Adventures of Ideas* (Macmillan, 1933), pp. 64-65.

and speech? My purpose in doing so is simple enough. I am seizing on a passage from one notable philosophic treatise to show that freedom—basic in Whitehead's thinking as it was in Lincoln's—finds its justification in the ends free men envisage and achieve in "man's vast future."

No need to accept Whitehead's philosophy as a whole, or any completed metaphysics or theology, in order to sense the fact that democracy is but at its beginnings when it overthrows the tyrant. The "consent of the governed" must be more than a consent to garner increasing stores of "consumer's goods," each person for himself. It is not certain that atomic power, "lifting the yoke of labor from the worn neck of the race," will thereby improve the human breed. Justice Holmes called the Biblical injunction, "Whatsoever thy hand findeth to do, do it with thy might" the most important message of the Book. Much depends on what atomic power leaves for men to do, and what they do it *for*.

The deepest fault of communism turns out to be its denial of freedom—a denial in the name and for the sake of a godless equality of material possession. But democracy may have as deep a fault if it fails to make freedom productive of a common life that is not tarnished by divisive superiority, close kin to the spirit of slavery. Democracy calls for a common life which is not

sordid, ruthless, mean, or ugly. "The last best
hope of earth" implies a vision beyond "live and
let live," a vision which in some sense has "persuasive beauty" for everyone who catches glimp-
ses of its meaning.

If this should seem to put too great a strain
upon the word "democracy," perhaps I ought to
use a less restrictive term, say, democratic *civi-
lization*. But for America, and for American education, my contention would remain the same:
freedom must meet the challenge of inspiring
human beings to make their life together *better*.

Better than what? Better than it is or may become in countries that have bartered freedom
for security; better than it is today in America;
better in every dimension by which life can
properly be measured; better, above all, in a life
that is lived in common sympathy, common
effort, a common search for excellence, and
common reverence.

Bound up with the idea of democracy as the
last best hope of earth is the conception that
human beings can become more than nature
made them. Man is not an animal, to be "condi-
tioned" to a "brave new world" which rulers
have devised, in which the common herd is held
to labor by deceit, by lies about surrounding
foes, by constant fears, by shutting out the mystic
element on which the possibility of human

brotherhood is based. Looking at the question with an open mind, can we doubt that men's trust in one another has its deepest foundation in their response to an ideal; and that their dignity as men depends upon it, also? What does the worth of the individual amount to except as it is measured by men's power to reach out beyond themselves toward understanding and toward partnership in some advancement of humanity?

"Communism," writes Adlai Stevenson, "knows no God and cannot satisfy the hungry heart." From Marx to Khrushchev, communism promises more land, more food, more jobs for everyone. That is a challenge to democracy. It is a challenge democracy cannot meet as communism meets it—by compulsion and slave labor. Nor can democracy content itself with full employment under living standards better than the communist countries manage to achieve, with all their use of terror. Democracy must cease to hold out as its only or its major hope that anyone who has ability in business—or the luck to hit upon a happy way to make and sell what everybody needs—can rise from rags to riches. The chance to make a fortune should never be excluded or derided; and of course it has already suffered limitations due to income taxes and related measures. What democracy can promise is not equality of possessions but, for rich and poor alike, the chance to move together, beyond material plenty, toward peace and mutual trust and common action for enlargement of the life that any of us leads.

Of course such words are empty to the starving. First things come first. But more to eat is not the end of what democracy proposes. "America the Beautiful" should be sung more often than it is; and schools, roads, churches, universities, libraries, hospitals, and many public services might be supported with less grumbling and resistance. The record of American philanthropy has been, since Carnegie, an inspiration; and American support of charitable causes is generous almost to a fault. But public understanding of the total vision which democracy implies leaves much to be desired.

Democracy implies an education which involves an understanding of ideals and hence is more than training, even if the training have behind it all the knowledge men can gain about the working of the human body, mind, and heart. If some, who know, who are the scientists, can tell us how to pull the strings, shall we proceed to pull them? If ends, including ends that are ideal, that draw from life's persistent mysteries, are not revealed through learning, then learners are condemned to learn but tricks. In education for

democracy we cherish the inviolable hope that
people, given opportunity—and granting everything that may be said about their differences as
individuals, including differences that lead to
jail or other institutional care—can, in their common life, be more than puppets.

It is plain enough that leadership is needed;
but the vision of the leaders must be shared. The
sharing, to be sure, presents a problem, both for
given times and given populations, and indeed
for given visions.[3] But if ideals remain unshared,
they are either ineffective, hugged to the bosoms
of the elect and withering in a petty circuit of
experience, or else they are imposed—and so drop
down to what can be imposed without inducing
a rebellion.

In any case the ancient riddle stands: *Quis
custodiet ipsos custodes?* The guardians of the
people can find no guardian but in ideals the
people share—or can be helped to share.

Or if the guardian appeals to science, then, as
scientist, he must defend his right to use his
knowledge for the ends he happens to perceive—
and so explain himself; which makes him party
to the never-ending search for worthier goals
for living. The scientist who works for truth or
dies for it, as many have, confesses to a faith. At

---

[3]I know of no profounder analysis of this problem than
Whitehead's, in Part I of *Adventures of Ideas*.

some point science yields to insight into values, as Kant maintained, and Royce, and James, and Whitehead, and our own beloved Robert Ulich, for all their philosophic differences; and as the great religions urge. "When me they fly, I am the wings," wrote Emerson, in "Brahma," a poem on the philosophic mind.

Let no one take this statement to imply distrust of science nor dismissal of its claim to give us surer knowledge of the facts of human nature and behavior. As a most convincing instance, take the work on juvenile delinquency so ably done by Drs. Sheldon Glueck and Eleanor Glueck. They show us where to work, how much to hope for, and the most effective agencies and methods to employ. Nor do they let the facts they give us blast the hope that human hearts and minds may still be open, in the main, to motivations higher than self-interest. The problem, as they have revealed it, leads to education —in its largest sense and scope.

For human beings are not *born* with insight into values, nor with understanding of the problems to be solved if values higher than their own survival are to be attained. What are the ends worth working for from day to day, worth dying for if need be, to be sought by common effort in a democratic order which can be called with truth "the last best hope of earth"? What prob-

lems are so basic in democracy that "*all* Amer-
can youth" should understand them in their
general bearing on our future as a people or the
future we should stand for in the world?

In years past, I have not found the answers I
have searched for to these questions in our educational literature in general. Now, I think they
have appeared, at least in their robust beginnings.
They have been only hinted at in histories where
I have sought them, such as Toynbee's monu-
mental *Study*, or the books of Truslow Adams or
the Beards. I have found more discouragement
than hope in the works of many publicists,
especially those who have most to say about our
schools. The answers that merit belief enough to
try them out seem to me to come from recent
books and from trends in educational practice
that are young enough to be disorganized and
groping, like the waving of a baby's arms before
he gets his fingers in his mouth.

Thus far in this address, I have sought only to
express a point of view. Democracy is the at-
tempt to bring people together, not only to act
by majorities on present issues, but to work out,
in freedom, in fairness to one another, with a
sense of their brotherhood as human beings, ways
of life that are better than any known or now
foreseen. Democracy implies a sharing, to the

fullest possible extent, in whatever men can do together to improve the human situation. There shall be no exclusions of any who are capable of taking a constructive part, whatever it may be. As talents vary, services must vary; and understanding of ideals will vary; and also power to comprehend the problems to be met; and in the end, capacity to act upon them.

But the vision must be shared; and if, for us, its surest messenger is religion, I believe the schools can take a vital part in rendering the vision more compelling. Democracy is therefore linked to our religious life, as Lincoln felt it was; but not to any single creed or institutional religious body, for freedom fails its final test unless it lifts external pressures to adhere to an established church. The link between religion and democracy is in their reference to the future and the faith that men can work together in response to deeper urges than their natural hungers or their will to power.

This outlook, I contend, need not ignore immediate and very practical considerations. It need not be abandoned in the face of present fact. It can be mingled into our approach to education without committing us to doubtful doctrines as to man's inherent goodness. It is not based on sentimental optimism. It calls for courage. Human lownesses and losses may be absolute, in spite of agencies that try to save the "down and out." The schools have taken on a longer fight.

I close this section, therefore, with the words of William James, at the end of his essay called "Is Life Worth Living?"

I confess that I do not see why the very existence of an invisible world may not in part depend on the personal response which any one of us may make to the religious appeal . . . For my own part, I do not know what the sweat and blood and tragedy of this life mean, if they mean anything short of this. If this life be not a real fight, in which something is eternally gained for the universe by success, it is no better than a game of private theatricals from which one may withdraw at will. But it *feels* like a real fight,—as if there were something really wild in the universe which we, with all our idealities and faith-fulnesses, are needed to redeem; and first of all to redeem our own hearts from atheisms and fears . . .

These, then, are my last words to you: Be not afraid of life. Believe that life *is* worth living, and your belief will help create the fact. The "scientific proof" that you are right may not be clear before the day of judgment (or some stage of being which that expression may serve to symbolize) is reached. But the faithful fighters of this hour, or the beings that then and there will represent them, may then turn to the faint-hearted, who here decline to go on, with words like those with which Henry IV greeted

the tardy Crillon after a great victory had been
gained: "Hang yourself, brave Crillon! We fought
at Arques, and you were not there." [4]

II

The heritage expressed for us by Lincoln and
preserved for us by him and by his generation is
beset today by perils he could hardly have fore-
told. Government of the people, for the people,
by the people has not perished from the earth;
and in the ninety years since Lincoln died, democracy has been sustained in two world wars:
yet never has it known so stark a challenge as it
faces now.

This statement, I assume, need not be argued,
despite the peace and quiet which surround us
here. But what these perils are and what the
schools can do to meet them should be argued
among teachers far more often than it is.

If Alexander Inglis were alive today, I think
he would agree that American secondary education is confronted with a new emergency. He
did not fail to call attention to the duty of our
schools to aim at civic virtue and intelligence;

---

[4]William James, *The Will to Believe and Other Essays
in Popular Philosophy* (new edition, Longmans, Green,
1937), pp. 61–62.

but Inglis did not live to see how urgent is the need to concentrate on that objective. He lived through World War I, which revealed all too little of what was to follow and seemed, in the end, to make democracy safe enough—at least for the time being. And the United States could still think of itself as self-sufficient, leaving the League of Nations to struggle along under the old, unfruitful notion of a balance of power.

In 1924, were many of us asking how the schools could work to make "the American dream" so vital and so much more worthy— "with malice toward none, with charity for all" —that most Americans could see it clear, not for their own advantage or defense alone, but for humanity?

We face a wholly unexpected combination: communist imperialism and atomic weapons.

If there is in fact "no alternative to peace," and if America must show "the courage to be patient," how many young Americans know all, or any major part, of what our own democracy must do, or keep from doing, in the long, hard, dangerous years ahead? The choice may be between one world, divided for a while, perhaps for many years—or darkness and destruction. "Situations of strength" from which democracy may negotiate, are not simply situations of superior armed power. If we have to fight for real estate in any corner of the world, we know we shall not fight to hold it for ourselves—the veriest chauvinist among us is aware of that. Nor can we purchase safety for ourselves merely by buttressing democracies or near-democracies— or even "friendly" nondemocracies—against encroaching communism. Beyond defense there is the business of giving to democracy at home and elsewhere the internal spiritual strength to live and grow. As teachers, how shall we address ourselves to that?

Of course we have to think of our defense against aggression and the rooting out of Reds of various complexions here at home; but scare headlines and Congressional investigations have emphasized these matters out of all proportion. The schools should offer more perspective, nearer to the wide and balanced view, as open as the prairie or the sea, which Lincoln put before our forbears in an earlier time of trial.

When communist aggression or subversion flares too fiercely in the foreground of our thoughts, we may be struck by panic and, like people in a burning house, pick up some trivial thing to save. Our gadgets and our customary comforts and amusements sometimes seem to be our choicest treasure. Are we bent on safety and security, and nothing more? Or is it just survival that we want, with the vague hope of keeping, somehow, what we have acquired? The easiest way to that result might be appeasement. And we can not forget that the communist appeal is full of promises, especially to those who have not caught the meaning of democracy or find themselves excluded from its benefits because of prejudice, mismanagement, or freedom exercised in ruthlessness. Asking a boy to die for freedom —or even to be drafted for it—is a test of what we mean by freedom.

Again and again we have been reminded that democracy is a goal for our lives in peace as well as an aim for our arms in war. General Dean has urged us to "present a factual world better than the communist dream" and "have political answers simple enough to understand . . ." Stevenson's *Call to Greatness,* Eisenhower's inaugural prayer, and the Supreme Court's decision on segregation in the schools can all be written into the same story. "It is for us, the living, . . . to be dedicated to the great task remaining before us . . ." Americans above all other peoples, have to *work* at freedom, which has never been a self-contained and independent goal, with nothing added as to what men do with it.

The communist threat is so massive and direct that it can be taken all too readily to mean only a power-conflict between Russia and the United States—the inevitable contest which de Tocqueville foresaw between the two colossi of the world to come. If we take the communist challenge to mean only that, we miss its wider import for the world and for ourselves. It is more than a threat of war. It is also a challenge to our thinking and our will to make democracy a living faith, a faith that works, at home.

The importunate details of daily living—its fun and friendships quite as often as its burdens and its sorrows—make it hard enough to focus thought and action on a national ideal, a kind of life we might be helping, in whatever measure, to achieve. Now the terrible shadow of a total war distracts us further. We need reminders that democracy is our business—a business that requires a deep patience, because it is the very nature of democracy to engender many and divergent definitions, many differences of emphasis and choices of means. Both the conception itself and the problems to be faced require new attention. The schools should be free to give them new attention, unless, as Robert Maynard Hutchins pointedly expresses it, we want our teachers to become "afraid to teach."

Not less do we need to be reminded that democracy is not a crown for us to wear, a scepter which entitles us to rule, or a bill of goods which we can export at a price. It is all too easy to think of democracy as if it were made up of our blessings, whether they are gifts of nature or the products of our labor, and then to look upon our blessings as if they were cleared lands in the encroaching jungle of desire on the part of millions who would take our blessings from us. Of course the problems of a world economy are complex almost beyond unraveling. So are the problems of international relationships, especially in Asia. Shall we therefore accept the communist contention that there is no issue in the world except between the have-nots and the haves?

The principles of democracy work themselves out on a world scale as an effort to put men on their own feet, regardless of their color, creed, or station, wherever they may be, and to welcome new peoples into the human family as members in full standing, with opportunities which they themselves desire to have and which they have at least begun to show the will and power to use responsibly. Democracy calls on us and other nations bred in freedom to sympathize with the drive toward national independence when that is at stake and to help in the development of natural resources in other lands than ours. It bids us deny in ourselves the will to dictate or to dominate. Falling short of this, leaving us absorbed in our own protection, our democracy drops down to pettiness—and we have no business to parade our Declaration or our

Constitution or our adherence to the great principles formulated in the Charter of the United
Nations.

We still have to "do all that may achieve and
cherish a just and lasting peace among ourselves
and with all nations." We must grant sadly that
the first World War did not attain the end that
Woodrow Wilson set for our participation; nor
did the League when we failed to support it;
nor World War II; and we may be forced to go
on to admit with apprehension that the United
Nations may not do so, either: yet the march of
these events will come to failure only if democracy shrinks in upon itself and we, among the
leaders in democracy, give up thinking in the
broadest human terms.

Much of all this may verge upon the controversial—which is, I willingly admit, an under-
statement; but I am not asking schools to teach
the views of freedom and democracy I am ex-
pounding here nor teachers to accept them. Nor
am I asking citizens, or teachers either, to aim at
some impossible ideal, which might disrupt the
world. I am not suggesting that everyone can be
an Albert Schweitzer, though we all may thank
the Lord that Schweitzers do occasionally ap-
pear. What I ask is that the schools make way
for much discussion of democracy and much discussion of its problems. It is what the schools can

do in the face of present issues and conditions that concerns us here.

It is almost laughable to hold that schools can teach democracy without discussion. Activities are certainly important, but by themselves they may result in interest that is evanescent, disconnected, or unstable. Ceremonies count, but the patriotic fervor they arouse can yield to disillusionment and cynicism. Various "zeal for democracy" movements have not led us far beyond good attitudes which easily evaporate. And when we look at much of our teaching of history, geography, and "civil government," must we not admit that masses of fact can become a sodden weight, half learned or learned for momentary presentation only, if problems that are real and present do not draw them, like a magnet, into patterns? Discussion of problems is the very heart of the matter.

Discussion may lead far. I can not think that it will often lead so far, in schools, as Dr. Hutchins recommends—into the Great Conversation, as he calls it, on the nature and the fate of man.[5] But discussion of our national faith, the roots of it, the worth of it, the obstacles we face in holding to it—this would itself go far toward giving secondary education the content of ideas which

---

[5]Robert M. Hutchins, *The Conflict in Education in a Democratic Society* (Harper & Brothers, 1953), p. 9off.

Dr. Hutchins rightly says it often lacks. It could certainly bring perspective into the confusion of the day's events and lift the minds of boys and girls above the comics, sports, and crime.

Of course school work has always called for problem-solving; and the notion that all learning develops "mental muscle" will not down, in spite of much discrediting. But the problems here in view are of a different order, for which but scanty preparation is afforded by the "mental discipline" of ordinary learning; and only recently have teachers started to work out ways to handle them successfully. They are issues still unsettled, on which the world outside the school still stands divided. In one way or another, all of them are controversial. But by so much the more are they worth thinking about. If our schools ignore them, let us give up claiming that we offer education which "prepares for life" or even trains a boy or girl "to think."

The air we breathe is full of raucous voices, cheap music, vulgarities, and the mouthings of demagogues. Can the school offset these influences simply by insistence upon purity of language, discipline of thinking about abstractions, and exactness in the learning of undifferentiated facts?

Not one of these insistences would I decry, except the last; but I maintain that something

more is needed. I am not urging anything the
schools have never heard of, nor a strange new
method, nor a "course" that must be crowded
into a curriculum already crowded. I ask a different question: Is there no room in schools as
they now operate—or as they could be brought
to operate without a revolution—for discussions
under many teachers of many subjects, in many
classrooms, homerooms, playing fields, and
offices, of what democracy means and what its
problems are?

Having put this question, may I turn aside now,
to come at it again, after a backward glance at
trends in educational thinking and how the
schools have followed them—or tried to?

III

My recollection of American educational
movements goes back over half a century. I hope
this audience won't regard me with remote
respect on that account, as one who "once saw
Shelley plain." On one occasion I was welcomed
in a company of book men at a Boston conven-
tion as if I were a ghost or a portrait of some past
worthy suddenly come to life—and all because,
quite inadvertently, I admitted having written,
back in 1912, two of the essays in the volume of

lectures which goes with President Eliot's "five-foot shelf" of books, the so-called Harvard Classics.

Yes, I knew and studied with James, Royce, Palmer, Santayana, and later worked with President Eliot, William Alan Neilson, and Alfred North Whitehead. I have talked at some length with Dewey and Thorndike. I have known personally Hanus, Cubberley, Flexner (still active in good works at 89), and most of the other men who have given these Inglis Lectures; also most of the men whose photographs Professor J. L. Meriam gave to our school in 1945—more than a hundred leading American "Contributors to Education" whom Meriam himself had known. This is not the place or time, however, for personal reminiscences; so let me make bold to offer a generalization out of remembrance of times past.

Almost all the educational movements I have witnessed sprang from one soil or drew their strength from it. I mean the pressure of a rapidly increasing population on our schools. I used to meet the harsher critics of our secondary education with what I called "a song of sevens": In 1870 there were 70,000 pupils in our public high schools; 70 years later there were nearly 7,000,-000; soon we had about 700 junior colleges. Neither these nor more exact statistics are required to remind you of a situation none of us can possibly escape. These mounting numbers put before us a new problem—a problem not of buildings or finances only but of what to teach and how.

What shall we do with pupils who prove them-selves to be, by all our customary methods, hard to educate? Swift's "short way with dissenters" has no more meaning in the premises than Marie Antoinette's "let them eat cake." Neither does "education for the gifted," which is only a part of the problem, important though it is. In fact, if handled without caution, education for the gifted might involve so sharp a separation of our pupils into sheep and goats that it would untimately compound our difficulties.

Of course much social theory, merging into educational theory, has done its part in making American schools the people's schools, instead of schools for a selected group. So have legal enactments as to school attendance; so has mounting wealth more evenly distributed (here I think of Frederick Lewis Allen's *The Big Change*); and recently the G.I. Bill of Rights. Even my scattered knowledge of the pertinent literature, from *The Federalist* papers through Veblen to T. V. Smith, Lippmann, and a score of others, could offer evidence (but you would have no time to listen if I tried to gather it to-

gether) that the problem which has vexed the
theorists is the problem which is burdening you:
what to do with the flood of young people who
used to leave school for jobs in their early teens
or before—and try (a few of them) to climb
Horatio Alger's ladder to success. Now they
can get the jobs no longer, and the schools must
take them all. If they were all "book-minded,"
the problem would be relatively simple. But
many learn from texts in common use with little
eagerness or profit. We have to keep them in
our classrooms in the hope that schooling will
absorb their energies. We have to put before
them something they can grasp and think about.
We have to help them, if we can, to choose constructive work and get some training for it.
Most of all, we have to inspire them to "get on
in life" and show them how to do it decently, or
even "justly, skilfully, and magnanimously," as
Milton expected of his "gentle and noble youth"
who were to be educated to do everything.

What educational movement can you think
of that is not rooted in some way in these considerations? Vocational education is, in all its
phases; home economics; the junior high school
and the junior college; opportunity schools; the
child-study movement and educational psychol-
ogy in general, from G. Stanley Hall to the behavioral sciences of today; progressive education

in several of its aspects; health education, at least in part; educational measurement; studies of the learning process, especially in reading; the raising of standards and expansion of facilities for the professional preparation and certification of teachers; education for family life; the current gropings after "life adjustment" education; the rise of the social studies; consumer education, expanding into economic education; education for intergroup understanding and good will; and now a new and mounting concern for civic education as a whole, to be connected somehow with education for moral and spiritual values.

The only "educations" I can think of which seem to be largely disconnected with the function of the schools in helping our entire American population to become American are safety education and aviation education: no doubt they too are needed but they are peculiarly *ad hoc*— as applicable, perhaps, in Moscow as in Washington.

In listing all these trends I did not set out to make anybody's head whirl, though my own has whirled a little as I did it. And even so, I have not mentioned educational administration with its train of problems in the building, staffing, and financing of the schools in cities, towns, and regions; nor the trying life of superintendents, facing elected school committees who want

good schools but are reluctant to call for the
taxes needed to pay for them; nor educational
surveys. Shades of the salary schedule and the
warrant for a new bond issue! These, too, pursue
us because Americans "know of no safe depository of the ultimate powers of society but
in the people."

Is the situation in the schools and in the study
of education so burdensome and complicated
that something must give way? No doubt there
must be changes all along the line, but that is
altogether normal. Looking back, I gain in confidence, because I see that in a period of immense
and rapid change in everything outside the
schools—technology, business organization, social
relations, and world conditions—our teachers and
their professional leaders, backed by enlightened
and determined citizens, are trying to help the
schools continue to serve basic needs, in spite of
all confusions and bewilderments. There is ferment in education because there is ferment and
tension in the world. I am not afraid that teachers
will "throw out the baby with the bath."

What will help most, as I see the total situation, both in retrospect and as it stands today, is
more concentrated attention, leading to bolder
experiment, on *what* to teach: I mean the actual
choice of subject matter in detail—ideas and problems and supporting facts. There are innumerable

things that are "nice" to know. Colleges have
stopped asking for so much "polite learning,"
but they seem to have put little in its place beyond some evidence of quickness of mind. What
must young Americans know—not by learning
pat answers from a book but by having experi-
ences and discussing problems central to the life
they soon must enter?

I am back at my main question: Can we not
find room in schools for more discussions of democracy and of its problems? The educational
movements I reviewed so rapidly lead up to this
inquiry. Chiefly in vocational education, long
established as a going concern, and later in the
development of the social studies and their very
recent emphasis on problems of our public life,
seen in the light of what democracy requires,
do I discern a trend toward thinking *through*—
away from peripheral questions as to methods,
means, facilities, processes, and stages of growth,
toward central questions as to what it is we simply *have* to teach.

How do we pick out subjects, topics, facts,
habits, skills, attitudes, or ideals which *must* be
taught, not to a few but to all who can learn—
and at public expense if not otherwise, under state
leadership wherever, as in Massachusetts, it can
be legally established?

Much may be taught to the few because in

their hands it will have fruitfulness for many:
you and I need not know Latin, yet I would
defend the teaching of it in the public schools—
but only to selected groups and chiefly in the
hope that Gibbonses, Rostovtzeffs, and Toynbees
need not vanish from the earth. But what should
be taught to everyone, whether he or she will
ever read Toynbee or not? That question seems
to me the most decisive question democratic education has to face.

It is interesting to learn that the Society for
Supervision and Curriculum Development promises a yearbook on this question in 1956. I am
glad some organization in Education (with a
capital E) has decided to tackle it.

When President Eliot said in his Inaugural that
for the individual it is concentration, for the
state variety, he was talking in vocational terms,
in terms of callings, at the level of higher education. He was speaking of the fields of higher
learning (now we are calling them, with a mistaken implication, "disciplines") as tools required
in the higher vocations. "We want them all," he
said, "and at their best." But Eliot was too
strongly democratic—I am sure I could defend
this statement—to argue for required teaching
aimed entirely at private happiness. Eliot, as an
educator, was not concerned with personal de-
lights, to be cherished in the "dim, phantasma-

goric chamber of the brain, with the pictured window and the storied wall," which Robert Louis Stevenson recommended as a haven of escape from the "salts and acids" of reality. Eliot wanted Harvard College to send forth young men "to serve their country and their kind" in addition to, or by means of, their own advancement.

If Eliot subscribed to a restricted program for the schools, as he did in the "Report of the Committee of Ten," it was because he had not yet perceived the limits of the idea of "mental discipline." And who, in 1893, could see the problem facing us today—the entire body of American youth in school, the desperate need to bring out the meaning and promise of democracy against the pressures, tensions, and confusions of the life around us?[6]

But this must end my "backward glance." What do I make of it, in terms of present possibilities?

---

[6]I am indebted to my friend, Dr. Howard E. Wilson, for a reminder pertinent here: an education which helps to give social or public purpose to ordinary living might play a part in the rescue of many an individual from frustrations leading over into mental breakdown. Mental health has become a problem of unexpected and disturbing proportions. Whatever lifts attention to common issues and common goals would seem to look toward wholesomeness—and this without offense to any school of psychiatric thought!

IV

Here, then, I must offer an assessment of what is needed most of all:

First, discussion of the meaning of democracy. I mean discussion, not the memorizing of definitions. I mean discussion in English classes, history classes, language classes, vocational classes, guidance conferences, assemblies, hygiene classes, the gymnasium, the laboratory (if there is one), the art room, music room, and library. And of course in the class in problems of democracy. Make way for such discussions!

When I studied Virgil, no one told me the *Aeneid* was a poem in defense and celebration of the Roman Empire. I should not have learned less Latin if I had been led on to think of Rome in contrast to America. The tags of Latin I retained took on a civic meaning for me far too late— long after my first Harvard course in Latin, which was as innocent of civic reference as anything I learned in school.

Is mathematics—"mathematics for the masses" —devoid of opportunity to discuss democracy? What does our welfare program cost—and why maintain it? Perhaps the formulae that stump us all on Form 1040 are beyond all explanation, but some reference to income taxes would not be out of place in algebra. The organization I am working for at Tufts has a partially completed manuscript called "Mathematics for Civic Purposes."

And need I speak of opportunities in science—now, when the fate of freedom is so often hung on what the scientists discover and their willingness to tell us what it means?

Of course I do not say that every discussion of democracy should be a discussion of all there is to democracy. I have tried to suggest that democracy is so much more than a form of government that it leads over into inspirations closely akin to those of our Judaeo-Christian tradition. Somewhere, I should hope, but not on every occasion in every class, discussion of democracy as an ideal could go that far. It will, in certain cases, if it is not halted by a lesson-setting, examination-driven, public-criticism-fearful complex.

Second, discussion of selected problems of democracy—"key" problems, political, economic, and social. Of course they must be problems which can be discussed in secondary schools. Let us admit that high-school teachers, even with their very brightest pupils, should hesitate to tackle certain problems of democracy; and some of these may hide in their complexity the turning points on which success or failure for democracy may hinge. In that case, what we have to teach is trust in experts—which is itself a lesson in democracy, not to mention the processes by which experts are selected, trained, and held accountable.

International finance occurs to me as an example of a problem we must leave to specialists. I choose it, you will guess, because I find it quite incomprehensible myself. Perhaps our friends who are working exclusively at economic education can make it simple enough for me, and so for high-school classes. However that may be, there are other problems that are crucial to democracy and yet fully subject to discussion in a high-school class.

Labor-management relations is one; the fundamentals of a free economy, not forgetting its social obligations or its difficulties, constitute another, or many others; and then follow (but in no fixed sequence) political reform in town and city government; civil rights in law and practice; public opinion and its sources in the press and mass-communication media; how to know a good political candidate when you see him; how communities can get to work to meet their own needs; what youth can do, with adult help, toward checking lawlessness; the conservation of natural and human resources; and how the isms differ from democracy. This is not an ordered

list nor a complete list. If I offered an ordered
list, you might think I intended to set up a program, grade by grade, or in a single course, to
cover everything. The time for that has not
arrived. Maybe it never will. Nevertheless I believe programs can be worked out which will be
in a substantial sense "full-fledged"; but they
will be and ought to be subject to change to fit
local conditions, so long as the major aims are
not forgotten or obscured.

The major aim is, first of all, a clearer grasp
and deeper faith in democracy. After that, and
helping to achieve it, aims like these: a keener
interest in politics; a more determined effort to
choose superior political leaders; firmness against
prejudice and the denial of civil rights to any
group or class; respect for law and a stronger
sense of its dependence upon community support; willingness to help in community improvements; a surer understanding of our economic
system; a larger outlook on the international
situation, with its central issue between war and
peace in an atomic age; and finally a more abid-
ing confidence in the value of religious inspiration not only in our private lives but in our civic
living.

I will not say these aims cover all that may or
should be done in civic education. They do seem
to me to form a fairly comprehensive set of ob-

jectives, interwoven one with another, and not vitiated by making one aim—even so important an aim as intergroup understanding, respect, and good will—stand out as separate from all other aspects of good citizenship.

Of course the question will arise, "But how can teachers undertake all this?" The answer, though it is not obvious, is hardly far to seek. In their college studies, teachers ought to come to grips with major social issues, and in their special preparation for their work as teachers become acquainted with the aims, materials, and methods of education for citizenship. This is a dual requirement I would urge for all teachers, not for social-studies teachers only; but of course the social-studies teachers should do more than others.

Meanwhile, and for years to come, there will be need for materials which teachers can use immediately, coöperatively, and successfully to arouse interest in civic issues, stimulate enthusiasm for a democratic attack on the civic faults and weaknesses common to American life, and bring out both difficulties to be overcome and the hope of overcoming them.

To establish adequate programs of civic education in every American school system is a massive undertaking. I do not subscribe to the idea that we need a more godlike breed of teachers to get very far with it. It is unrealistic to suppose we shall have a total group of teachers far superior to those in office now. The improvements we need in American schools, from higher pay and smaller classes to greater respect for the teacher's position, will enable teachers who have the necessary training to do amazing things. And even without some or all of these improvements, teachers are forging ahead in many places now.

Here I have been talking, of course, out of my own "shop"—the Civic Education Center at Tufts University. I am sure you will forgive me for that. Let me close, except for a paragraph or two which reverts to my opening section, with a listing of certain volumes—not many, and none of them exhaustive or exhausting tomes—which will sustain my argument in one way or another. Like a Congressman whose speech is too long— or too dull—to finish on the floor, I "beg leave to print." I put these references before you in chronological order, with a note on each. They do not constitute a library on education for democracy, or even a five-foot shelf; but anyone who reads these books with care can hardly fail to see, I should suppose, how they build up into a new demand on education.

1930: *The Great Investment*. The Inglis Lecture, by Thomas H. Briggs. Cambridge, Mass.: Harvard University Press.

Beware of interpreting Dr. Briggs's references
to the State as if Briggs meant that education
should support the State regardless of its nature
or its aims. See especially page 97.

1932: *Dare the Schools Build a New Social
Order?* A John Day Pamphlet, by George S.
Counts.

The title of this little volume suggests, unfortu-
nately, that Dr. Counts desires to exchange democracy for some new form of government or
life. Per contra, he is seeking ways to help democracy fulfill its basic promises and premises.
See his peroration, pages 52–56.

1938: *Education for Citizenship,* by Howard
E. Wilson. New York: The Regents' Inquiry,
The McGraw-Hill Book Co.

The first study, state-wide, of the civic results of
education not specifically directed toward civic
ends. It shows clearly what was not accomplished
in most schools and what some schools did accom-
plish because they made, in spite of handicaps, a
determined and clear-headed effort.

1940: *Learning the Ways of Democracy: A
Case Book of Civic Education.* Washington,
D.C.: Educational Policies Commission, National
Education Association of the United States and
the American Association of School Administra-
tors.

This notable early publication of the Educational Policies Commission has had good effect in helping teachers and school officers to establish a democratic atmosphere in schools themselves. It has little to say about discussion of current public issues; but teachers who do not know it have missed a book of basic and continuing value.

1945: *For Us the Living: An Approach to Civic Education*, by John J. Mahoney. New York: Harper & Brothers.

I can not comment on this book with impersonal calm. It spoke to me with the tongue of angels—and therefore upset all my plans for philosophic writing at my ease in my declining years. A bit shamefacedly I mention the fact that during my classmate's and colleague's years of labor on the book, which has become the vade mecum of our joint enterprise since 1948, I did write a few things myself which were not without relation to his far more effective analysis.

1946: *Education and World Tragedy*, by Howard Mumford Jones, Cambridge, Mass.: Harvard University Press.

The first clear statement, so far as I can tell, as to the consequences for education of the new and fearful state of world affairs.

1952: *Education for Citizenship*. A Report to the Commissioners of Education of the Northeastern States. Published out of a grant from the

Edward A. Filene Good Will Fund, and to be obtained from Commissioner John J. Desmond of Massachusetts.

> This is a compact but conprehensive account of the aims, curriculum, temper, and community relationships of schools that would move toward actual results in "civic virtue and intelligence."

1954: *Educating for Citizenship*. The 32nd Yearbook of the American Association of School Administrators.

> I doubt if this volume omits anything of practical importance as to what is needed and what has so far been attempted in civic education in this country.

To some of you this list will lead to background reading, unless you have already covered much of it, perhaps without conclusions as to what to do about it. John Dewey's *Democracy and Education* should be supplemented by Robert Ulich's *Conditions of Civilized Living* and his *The Human Career;* and for background of another sort, I recommend Carl J. Friedrich's *New Image of the Common Man*, Ralph Barton Perry's *The Citizen Decides*, and James Bryant Conant's *Education and Liberty: The Role of the Schools in a Modern Democracy*. An admirable statement of what our schools have done and are doing for America is the latest publication of the

Educational Policies Commission—*Public Education and the Future of America.*

I think also of two books which will give you arguments against what I am arguing for. Sir Richard Livingstone's *On Education* despairs of doing anything important in the schools. He believes the minds of young people can be plastered with a few facts and disciplined to a few desirable skills and habits, but not brought to grips with problems and ideas of any civic pith or moment. He urges adult education as our only hope. I would say to Sir Richard that you never can tell till you try; but I would join him in strong advocacy of adult education.

Dr. Robert Maynard Hutchins' book, to which I have already referred, seems to me to be too condemnatory of education which takes its inspiration from the need for social reform. I would agree with Dr. Hutchins, however, in his more recent article, called "Are Teachers Afraid to Teach?" in which he condemns the widespread public attitude toward teachers who deal with controversial problems. If education touches nothing that is controversial, how can it encourage thinking? Of course no teacher who understands what teaching means will raise a controversial issue and then lay down the law about it. Neither will he act as if he had no opinion of his own—although he may be excused, or even praised, for not having made up his mind on many a problem that is thorny. One opinion, however, every American teacher should hold and constantly reveal and exemplify—the opinion that the democratic way of working out a problem can be trusted and must be tried.

I will go no farther back in time nor outward into social theory, nor at all into behavioral science, that newest field in which the human mind hunts for itself outside itself. What these problems, aims, and books suggest is that we turn without unnecessary hesitation, especially in time of danger, to new selections of materials to teach, if only at a venture.

Four pioneering ventures in selection of ideas and issues to be taught I can not fail to mention, although I must not, since I am at work in one of them, make comparisons among them—nor do I wish to do so, for all four are working at a single, central problem.

The Joint Council on Economic Education, initiated in 1948 at New York University under the leadership of Dr. G. Derwood Baker, I have already referred to by implication. The council, a nonprofit, educational organization which has the support of the Committee for Economic Development and a distinguished Board of Trustees, operates chiefly through workshops for teachers, with frequent participation by pupils in secondary schools. Out of these workshops have come many reports of great interest, which the council distributes at cost from its headquarters, 2 West 46th St., New York 36, New York. The council has demonstrated that the economic issues of our democratic society can be understood and discussed straightforwardly and hopefully by American young people of varied background.

The Council for Advancement of Secondary Education, Inc., initiated by Dr. Thomas H. Briggs, sponsored by the National Association of Secondary School Principals, and supported by the National Better Business Bureau, is intent on identifying pertinent and teachable subject matter in the whole civic area, with first attention to the area of economics. Its present study of economic problems is directed by Dr. Galen Jones. Much may be expected of it.

The Citizenship Education Project of Teachers College, Columbia, directed by Dr. William S. Vincent and handsomely financed by the Carnegie Corporation, has identified nearly one hundred "premises" of democracy, and has published them in a synopsis called *When Men Are Free* (Houghton Mifflin, 1955). With this book the project offers an extensive bibliography of reading for teachers and a collection of activities for pupils called "laboratory practices." It has enlisted a very large number of state and local educational systems in carrying out its program.

The Civic Education Center at Tufts University has produced sixteen pamphlets on civic topics and published ten of them. The National Council for the Social Studies approves and distributes these materials. The pamphlets—for example, *Work Without Strife*, which deals with labor-management relations—are meant to be so thoroughly interesting, so simply worded, yet so unbiased and truthful, that discussions and activities can build on them toward fuller understandings and a reasonable hope that democratic action can work out answers better than we have at present. Guides for teachers are in preparation.

I have called these undertakings "ventures," and indeed they show a certain boldness. Their assumption is that teachers can and will presume to bring up in their classes problems that are controversial. This means that teachers must find ways to deal effectively with problems still debated in the press and elsewhere—ways of dealing with such problems which will make them real and interesting and vital to their pupils without arousing public fury or developing suspicion and mistrust from which the schools will suffer. As yet we have no measures of success in these attempts, nor do we know how deep or permanent their effects may be on pupils in the schools and classes where they have been—or yet may be—undertaken. By way of guidance, I can offer here no more than rules of thumb derived from observation and reports.

To start with facts, go on with facts, and end with facts, expecting pupils to make up their minds because they know the answers given by the facts, is fatal. The facts may not provide an answer. If they did, the problem would not long remain a problem. In any case, the problem must be broached in human terms. A story may be better than a table of statistics. If the story seems to draw a moral or conclusion that is over-simplified, then discussion, further reading, films, activities, and more discussion can correct the balance. Initial interest in the human meaning of the problem is a first essential.

It is just as fatal to be overcareful not to let the hope of ever finding answers enter into the proceedings. Suppose the problem is disarmament, to which a 12th-grade class has come from previous work on the United Nations. Of course the hopes of those who see disarmament as possible—and, in the end, the only way to lasting peace—must be offset by every rational objection urged against it. But the hopeful view should not be cast aside to die; indeed, it may be best to give it emphasis, without exaggeration of its possibilities.

One hope, as I have said, should never be obscured—the hope that in the democratic process of discussion answers may be found. If that should seem to be "indoctrination," then let us all be guilty of it!

The mountains of educational thinking have risen high in the half century since I first looked closely at their smaller, barer slopes. It is my honest conviction that their present labor has brought forth, in the new movement for civic education, something bigger than a mouse!

V

Here at the end of this address I must return to an idea implied in what I said at the beginning. Democracy, we are told, is based upon the notion that the individual is of eternal value in himself. On the scale of eternity, I would not dissent from that idea; nor on an earthly scale would I contest the doctrine of inalienable rights, to be preserved, defended, and made equally available or applicable to all. But the individual can forswear his rights by criminal acts, even his right to life, if his offense is rank enough. Not less surely can the individual sacrifice by what he does the trust, respect, and free coöperation of his fellow men.

Nor is coöperation in itself the hallmark of democracy. Mobs can coöperate. Masses can be swayed by panic—or just the sudden chance to flout the law. Witness the recent rioting in Montreal, where hockey "fans" (our dangerous shortening of the word *fanatics*) got out of hand.

Mass man is not the man democracy depends on or would aim at in its education. The rights democracy insists on are the rights of individuals who coöperate for ends beyond their own advantage, the advantage of their clan, or even of the nation as a means to what they want as individuals.

There is a sonnet by the great Catholic poet of the nineteenth century, Gerard Manley Hopkins, which offers in its first eight lines a wonderful celebration of individuality—of what it means to be a *self*. Then in the last six lines it pictures selfhood which responds to something more and other than self-will. The poetry of Hopkins is often unintelligible—at least to me; but in this sonnet, as in other poems, it rises to a beauty unmatched in its kind and has a moving power to put large meaning into little space. This sonnet has no title:

As kingfishers catch fire, dragonflies draw flame;
As tumbled over rim in roundy wells
Stones ring; like each tucked string tells, each hung bell's
Bow swung finds tongue to fling out broad its name;
Each mortal thing does one thing and the same:
Deals out that being indoors each one dwells;
Selves—goes itself; *myself* it speaks and spells,
Crying *What I do is me: for that I came.*

I say more: the just man justices;
Keeps grace: that keeps all his goings graces;
Acts in God's eye what in God's eye he is—
Christ—for Christ plays in ten thousand places,
Lovely in limbs, and lovely in eyes not his
To the Father through the features of men's faces.